26

W9-CNA-090

I love reading

Dinosaur Hunting
by Leonie Bennett

Consultant: Luis M. Chiappe, Ph.D.
Director of the Dinosaur Institute
Natural History Museum of Los Angeles County

BEARPORT
PUBLISHING

NEW YORK, NEW YORK

Credits

Cover, Title Page: Corbis; 4: Lisa Alderson; 5, 8, 9, 18B: Corbis; 7, 10, 11, 12, 14, 15, 16, 18T, 20–21, 22T, 23, 24: Shutterstock; 13, 22B: Robin Carter; 17, 19: Luis Rey.

Every effort has been made by ticktock Entertainment Ltd. to trace copyright holders. We apologize in advance for any omissions. We would be pleased to insert the appropriate acknowledgments in any subsequent edition of this publication.

Library of Congress Cataloging-in-Publication Data

Bennett, Leonie.
  Dinosaur hunting / by Leonie Bennett.
    p. cm. — (I love reading. Dino world!)
  Includes bibliographical references and index.
  ISBN-13: 978-1-59716-554-9 (library binding)
  ISBN-10: 1-59716-554-9 (library binding)
  1. Paleontologists—Juvenile literature. 2. Paleontology—Juvenile literature. 3. Dinosaurs—Juvenile literature. I. Title.

  QE714.5.B455 2008
  567.9—dc22

                    2007017849

Contents

Studying dinosaurs

Dinosaurs lived long ago.

Scientists called paleontologists study these animals.

Eoraptor
(*ee*-oh-RAP-tur)

paleontologists
(*pale*-ee-uhn-TOL-uh-jists)

Dinosaur fossils

Paleontologists learn about dinosaurs by looking at fossils.

Fossils are what is left of animals and plants that lived long ago.

This is a fossil of a dinosaur **skull**.

What does this fossil tell you about the dinosaur?

A paleontologist can tell it was a good hunter by looking at its jaws and teeth.

sharp teeth

strong jaw

How are fossils found?

This is Sam.

He is a paleontologist.

rock hammer

rock

Sam looks for fossils in rocks.

He digs the fossils out of the rocks very carefully.

Where are fossils found?

Fossils are found in lots of places.

Some fossils are found on the beach.

Others are found on top of mountains.

Fossils have been found all over
the world.

Finding fossils

When Sam finds a fossil, he does two things.

First, he writes down what the fossil looks like and where he found it.

fossil

Second, Sam draws a **map**.

It shows where each piece of the fossil was found.

map

What tools does Sam use?

Sam uses a rock hammer to get the fossils out of the rocks.

rock hammer

He uses small brushes to clean off sand and dirt.

brush

Sam also uses a computer to learn about the fossils he finds.

Studying a footprint

Sam can tell a lot from a **footprint**.

The dinosaur that made this one was very big.

dinosaur footprint

It walked on three toes.

Sam thinks it was an *Iguanodon*.

Iguanodon ate plants.

It was about 30 feet (9 m) long—almost as long as a school bus.

Iguanodon
(ih-GWAN-oh-don)

three toes

17

Studying a skull

Sam found this dinosaur skull.

It is very big!

The dinosaur had sharp teeth.

By looking at this fossil, Sam can tell that this dinosaur was a *Tyrannosaurus rex*.

sharp teeth

Tyrannosaurus rex
(ti-*ran*-uh-SOR-uhss REKS)

19

What happens to the fossils?

Most dinosaur fossils end up at museums.

Apatosaurus
(uh-*pat*-uh-SOR-uhss)

People who work at the museum
put the fossils together.

Now everyone can see the dinosaur's
skeleton!

Glossary

footprint (FUT-*print*) a mark made by a foot

map (MAP) a picture of where things are found

skeleton (SKEL-uh-tuhn) the framework of bones that protect or support the body

skull (SKUHL) the part of the skeleton that makes up the head

23

Index

Read More

Goldish, Meish. *The Fossil Feud: Marsh And Cope's Bone Wars.* New York: Bearport Publishing (2007).

Larson, Peter. *Bones Rock!: Everything You Need to Know to Be a Paleontologist.* Montpelier, VT: Invisible Cities Press (2004).

Learn More Online

To learn more about the world of dinosaurs, visit
www.bearportpublishing.com/ILoveReading